Supplement to
REVOLUTIONARY SOLDIERS
of
ONONDAGA COUNTY
NEW YORK

by

Rev. W. M. Beauchamp, S. T. D.

*Reprinted from
Annual Volume of the
Onondaga Historical Association
1914*

HERITAGE BOOKS
2011

HERITAGE BOOKS
AN IMPRINT OF HERITAGE BOOKS, INC.

Books, CDs, and more—Worldwide

For our listing of thousands of titles see our website
at
www.HeritageBooks.com

A Facsimile Reprint
Published 2011 by
HERITAGE BOOKS, INC.
Publishing Division
100 Railroad Ave. #104
Westminster, Maryland 21157

Originally published 1914

Annual Volume of the
Onondaga Historical Association

— Publisher's Notice —
In reprints such as this, it is often not possible to remove blemishes from the original. We feel the contents of this book warrant its reissue despite these blemishes and hope you will agree and read it with pleasure.

International Standard Book Numbers
Paperbound: 978-1-58549-827-7
Clothbound: 978-0-7884-8664-7

PREFACE

In 1913, Rev. Beauchamp compiled a book entitled *Revolutionary Soldiers Resident and Dying in Onondaga County, NY*. The work presented here represents additions and corrections to that work. The reader should be aware that the notes such as "See Salina", "See Tully" etc. refer one to the above compilation which is widely available having been reprinted in 1990.

The editor has taken some liberty with this "Supplement" by citing years as "1776" rather than '76 etc., although Rev. Beauchamp used both at various times. Names of Onondaga County towns have been spelled out rather than merely abbreviated. The editor also deleted slash marks inserted between words appearing in some tombstone inscriptions.

The reader will often find explanatory notes added to the text by the editor such as the location of a village or a further reference to consult. These annotations are made, through personal knowledge, as a long time resident of Onondaga and adjacent New York counties. These annotations are enclosed in brackets.

Rev. Beauchamp was anything but consistent in using abbreviations. As for example one finds Conn. in one place and Ct. in another; he would at times spell a word or name of a state completely and at other times use only an abbreviation. The present editor on occasion has substituted modern postal abbreviations of states. [MKM]

INTRODUCTION

It was expected that the list of local Revolutionary soldiers would gradually increase, and two things have already swelled it. Twelve names were omitted in the list furnished me from the Syracuse Post Office, and these are now added. In that list Jonathan is always changed to John. When the New York pension roll of 1835 was procured over eighty new names were added. Others came from other sources, but many will never be known.

All names are given alphabetically, even if uncertain, but the latter are designated. Some before suggest before are now certain. Some are repeated for needed addition or corrections. The list of 1835 gives service but not town of residence. That of the 1840 [census] reverses this. Reference here to a town is for the account in [the] preceding volume, but a mere mention is only for locality.

The pension list of 1835 is perplexing, intervals of years often separating applications for and and granting of pensions, nor do these agree with local records. In petitions it was customary to state the age, but there seem no rule in this list, yet it is thought best to give recorded ages with a caution as to use. In the list at large, hundreds of applications are said to have been made March 4, 1831, a very unlikely thing. In this county alone 130 are credited to that day. This list also throws light on the movements of veterans. Some went to other counties; some came here from them [other counties]. A few of these will be noticed.

Careful examinations have been made in the Surrogate's office, but only highly probable names have been retained, passing over some tempting records. It was hoped that the files of Mr. Redfield's early papers might be examined with good results, but while this could not easily be done, other journals have yielded much. Thus there will be future work for younger hands, for this supplement ends this line of research by the present compiler, now in his 85th year, a pleasant task, with all its vast amount of works.

Incidentally it should be said that pensioners were but a small fraction of those that served. [W.M.B.].

THE SOLDIERS

WILLIAM ABBE - (See Onondaga) This pensioner died Aug. 6, 1833. He applied for a pension in 1818 and his age is given as 75 years. In the 1835 list, however, his age is quite uncertain and dates of application by no mean agree with county records. In 1820, he was called 52 years of age.

AHIJAH ADAMS - (See DeWitt) This pioneers's name has been mis-spelled by writers. The prostate stone is broken through the name, but it is Ahijah, not Abijah and his story briefly follows. He was b. in Killingly, CT, Nov. 1858, dying in DeWitt Feb. 3, 1841 in his 83rd year. He settled there in 1794 on a soldiers claim, four miles east of Syracuse. When drafted for service, he engaged a substitute who lost his leg and afterward lived on and with him. He married (1) Lydia Cosgrove; (2)——; (3) Lydia (Hill) Granger in 1806; (4) Mrs. Hawks, April 1840 and had thirteen children.

JOHN ADAMS - (See Onondaga) There seems to be no doubt that both father and son were veterans. Major James H. Durham, of Cape Vincent, whose grandfather was a very early settler here, and whose wife was a descendant of both veterans visited the son in 1825, being then five years old. "I remember that my father said Deacon Adams was an old soldier. My father was an army officer himself and naturally would know about such matters."

ABIEL ALLEN - Camillus. Susannah Allen, admns., Jan. 18, 1808. Name in Mass., in Lexington Alarm and later. One from Worcester account in 1778, was then 22 years old. Of course in these letters of admns. age can only be conjectured, and so the list has carefully been condensed.

LEVI ALLEN - Application made March 4, 1831, his service being in Conn. Militia. His home was in Salisbury, and he was on an expedition against Ticonderoga in April-May 1775. Aged 77 yrs.

GIDEON ALLING - This veteran was born in Milford, Conn., March 16, 1774, served there and went to Marcellus in 1819, where he died Aug. 16, 1830. He married Sarah Russel July 11, 1782 who d. Sept. 25, 1833. Record in the family history.

POWELL J. AMMERMAN - Some of the Ammermans were buried in the Owasco cemetery, Skaneateles, as this veteran was, and others at Moravia, so that a reference to these and the Austins is conjectural. They are classed as Cayuga pensioners in 1835, but quite probably were buried in Onondaga Co.. Application made March 4, 1831, age 70 years. Served in the New Jersey Militia.

JOSIAH ANDREWS - See Fabius. Application 1831, age 81 yrs. Sergeant in Conn. Militia.

SAMUEL AUSTIN - Cayuga [Co.] pensioner, applied 1831 aged 84 yrs. Served in the Mass. militia. May have been buried in the Owasco cemetery in Skaneateles but this conjectural.

ZEPHANIAH AUSTIN - Cayuga pensioner, applied 1831, aged 71 years. Served in the New York Militia. See preceding [above] regarding burial.

JOY BABBITT - He applied for a pension April 13, 1818, from Lysander and again in 1820 in Ontario county, having enlisted in August 1782 in Capt. Williams company, Col. Sprout's Regiment, Mass. Line and went to the Hudson at once. In June 1783, he was transferred to Capt. Haskell's Co. and sent to Philadelphia. He was discharged in June 1784, he had left his discharge in Vermont. He was a fifer, aged 50 yrs. in 1818, and then living in Lysander. Born in Darmouth, Mass., Sept. 26, 1767, he died in Buffalo, NY, Nov. 7, 1849. He married Esther Cook, Sept. 16, 1786, who was born October 6, 1765 and died July 17, 1813. A second wife deserted him. Not in the rolls.

WILLIAM BACON - (See Onondaga) This pensioner applied in 1818, age 67 yrs. and served in the New York Line.

ENOCH BAILEY - (See Tully) Application in 1831, age 74 yrs. Served in the Conn. Militia.

CASPRUS BAIN - Applied 1831, age 74 yrs. Albany 10th regiment. In Argyle, NY in 1790.

JAMES BAKER - (See Marcellus) Applied April 11, 1818, age 68 yrs.

LEWIS BAKER - (See Marcellus) Served in NY Continentals.

JONATHAN BAKER - (See Marcellus) Applied 1819, age 59 yrs. [Served] in Mass. Line; came here from Rutland, Vermont.

NATHAN BAKER - Applied in Monroe County, Sept. 27, 1832, age 78 yrs. and had been a baptist elder. Enlisted under Capt. Thaddeus Lacey, Woodbury, CT in Col. Heman Swift's Regiment, June 1 - Dec. 1, 1776, serving mostly on Lake Champlain. In 1778 substituted for Phineas Baker for eight months, and was in the militia in 1779. In 1780 he was drafted, and in 1781 enlisted under Capt. Leavenworth. He was born in Woodbury, April 14, 1760, then [removed] to Washington county, NY; then was a year in Manlius and 32 [years] in Pompey, leaving there in 1828, and had been four years in Riga [Monroe CO.]. He does not appear in the list of 1840. Reported age placed birth in 1754.

BENONI BALLARD - Applied 1818, age 76 yrs. Died Aug. 10, age 76 yrs. Died Aug. 10, 1827. In 1st New York Line and Harper's Levies.

ANDREW BALSLEY - (See DeWitt) Applied in 1831, aage 76 yrs. In New York Militia.

HEARTWELL BARNES - (See Fabius) He died Sept. 11, 1820.

THOMAS BARNUM - Applied in 1831, age 81 yrs. Sergt. in the 12th Albany Regiment.

NICHOLAS BARTH - He was a lieutenant in the 1st Tryon Co. Regiment, Lieut. Col. Hyde, and was pensioned Oct. 7, 1786, a very early date.

NICHOLAS BARTLETT - (See Pompey) Applied 1831, age 85 yrs. Served in the Mass. Militia.

LEMUEL BATES - He was born in Brinfield [Brimfield?], Mass., March 4, 1847, going to Ohio after the war, On his return spent a short time in Syracuse, but died in Homer. He was a sergeant in Capt. Stoddard's Hampshire Militia in 1782, and married Farezinah Thompson, who died in Homer Aug. 3, 1852, age 98 yrs.

ZACHARIAH BEERS - Applied 1831, age 76 yrs. Sergeant in Capt. Nathan Hince's Militia company, Woodbury, CT. for one month in 1776.

JONATHAN BELDING - (See Onondaga) Applied 1831, age 73 yrs. Mass. Continentals.

SILAS BELLOWS - Salina. Elizabeth Bellows, admns., May 11, 1809. In Mass. Lexington Alarm and Saratoga. Probable.

JONATHAN BENEDICT - (See Pompey) Applied 1831, age 88 yrs. Sergt. in New York Militia.

DAVID BENNET - (See Van Buren) Thus [David] in 1835, but Daniel in 1840. The former is right. Applied 1831, age 70 yrs. In Capt. Prentice's company, Norwalk, CT in 1782.

PETER BERIAN, Sr. - Tully. Will made June 16, 1806; proved Feb. 23, 1807. Wife, Abigail. He left four sons and a married daughter. Name in 4th Regiment, Orange Co. In 1790 in Goshen, NY. Probable.

SAMUEL BERRY - Marcellus. Spencer Berry, admns., June 8, 1809. The latter died in 1811. Served in Mass. and New York. In 1790 [census?] Albany and Dutchess counties. Probable.

JACOB L. BEVIER - (Skaneateles) Cayuga pensioner, applied 1831, age 67 yrs. New York State troops.

JOSEPH BILLINGS - (See Skaneateles) The wife's inscription at Mottville is "Sarah, wife of Joseph Billings, died Aug. 4, 1836, aged 77 years."

HOOPER BISHOP - This Pompey pensioner was under Capt. John Carpenter, June 25 - Sept. 25, 1779; Capt. Caleb Keep, Oct. 18 - Nov 29, 1779 and in 1780 served from South Brimfield, Mass. age then 18, stature 5 ft. 5 in. Dark complexion. July - Dec. 1780 he was with Capt. George Webb at West Point. Applied in 1831 age 71 yrs. He went to Michigan where he died over a century old.

JOHN BISHOP - Applied 1818, age 79 yrs. Died Aug. 17, 1828. In New York Line.

ZENAS BLISS - Applied 1831, age 66 yrs. In Capt. Lovewell's company, VT Militia, July 1-Nov. 24, 1781.

JOHN BOOM - Lysander. Sally Boom and Joseph Cody, admns., June11, 1813. Under Col. Wynkoop and in the 1st NY Line, 1781. At Coxsackie in 1790. Probable.

JOHN BRIGGS - (See Skaneateles) Applied 1831 age 76. Age incorrect. In Conn. Militia. Capt. Ellsworth 1775; Capt. Dixon, 1776. Served from Sharon [CT] in 1781.

GIDEON BROCKWAY - In Camillus in 1807. Applied 1831, age 79 yrs. Served in Harper's New York Levies. In 1790 in Catskill. Died June 8m 1833.

JOHN BROOKS - Applied 1831, age 74 yrs. New York Continentals.

DANIEL BUNCE - (See Pompey) Died Dec. 10, 1823, age 7r yrs.

JOHN BURROUGHS - [Name was?] Buronough in 1835. Applied 1831, age 75 yrs. New York Militia. At first buried on his farm; [body] removed to Shephard Settlement in 1878.

JEREMIAH BURROUGHS - Marcellus. Will, Sept. 30, 1803 - March 30, 1804. Wife, Mary. Adult sons and married daughter. Name in 3rd New York Line. Probable.

DAVID BURTON - Applied 1831, age 88 yrs. In Capt. Abell's Company, Conn. Militia, 6 months in 1776. Prisoner at Fort Washington in that year.

EBENEZER BUTLER, Sr. - (See Pompey) In records of Branford, CT. Mrs. Minnie Kellogg (librarian in Syracuse Pub. Lib.) found that this veteran was born there Dec. 1, 1734 and married Miss Desire Barnes there March 30, 1757. Two of their children were born in that place, but Ebenezer, Jr. was born in Harwinton, CT, June 29, 1760. No previous record has been published with these dates, which correct some errors.

EBENEZER CALKINS - (See Manlius) In Lenox Rural Cemetery near Canastota [Madison Co.] are two stones, reading: Ebenezer Calking, died July 1, 1847 in the 83 year of his age." "Sally, wife of Ebenezer Calking, died Sept. 30, 1847, aged 66 years." This would be a second wife.

NATHAN CAMPBELL - Post office list. Capt. Ephriam Warren's company, Conn. Militia. In 1790 in Stephentown, NY, and Montgomery Co.. In 1807 [in] Camillus.

JACOB CARHART - Applied 1831, age 73 yrs. Weissenfels' New York Levies.

ISAAC CARPENTER - Pompey. Will, Sept. 23, 1807 - Mary 27, 1809. Wife, Jeane, with 5 sons and 3 daughters. Name in 14th Albany L. B. R. and in Orange 3rd L. B. R.. In 1790 [in] Goshen, NY. Probable.

RUFUS CARTER - (See Fabius) Applied 1831, age 69 yrs. Artificer in Conn. Militia.

GILES CASE - (See Onondaga) Applied 1831, age 76 yrs. Corporal in the New York Militia.

CALVIN CHAMBERLAIN - Onondaga. Simon Crandall, Paris, NY, admns., Dec. 12, 1806. Albany, 9th Regiment, L. B. R.

EPHRIAM CLARK - (See Pompey) In an abandoned cemetery 1 1/2 miles north of Pompey Center, are three inscriptions: "In memory of Ephriam Clark, who died Nov. 13th 1825, aged 72 years" and "Sarah, wife of Ephriam Clark, died Apr. 3, 1847, age 87 years & 7 months." [The 3rd inscription is not given here]. Probable.

JABESH HALL - "Died Apr. 21, 1826. aged 69 years, Lydia Hall, wife of Jabesh Hall, died June 24, 1843, aged 86 years" Lafayette cemetery. [He served in] Westchester Co., 4th Regiment. In 1790 Pawling, Dutchess county. Two of the name served in Massachusetts. Probable.

JAMES CLARK - Applied in 1831, age 78 yrs. Mass. Continentals. This pensioner differed greatly in age from one suggested as a probable soldier in Syracuse, but pension ages are not reliable. Two veterans seem probable.

LAMBERTON CLARK - Applied 1818, age 73 yrs. In Conn. Line under Capt. Warner, 1777 and a drummer under Col. Durkee in 1781. In Middletown in 1790, but came here from Vermont.

SAMUEL CLARK - See Manlius. Applied 1831, age 76 yrs. In Rhode Island Continentals.

SETH CLARK - See Otisco. Second epitaph should read "Hannah, wife of Seth Clark, died May 17, 1843 in th3 83rd year of her age."

BENJAMIN COATS - Applied 1831, age 83 yrs. In New York Militia.

AARON COE - Pompey. Brother of Ithamar. He was a capt. in Col. John Moseley's 3rd Hampshire Regt., Mass, 1776 and 1777. His brother was in the same regiment.

ITHAMAR COE - He was born in Durham, CT, Sept. 10, 1755 and removed to Granville, Mass. in 1775. He served Sept. 23 - Nov. 16, 1776 and July 9 - Aug. 12, 1777, in Hampshsire Co. Militia. He was an Ensign and enlisted in the Conn. Line July 10m 1780 being then 24 [yrs. of age], stature 5 ft. 7 inches and of light complexion. He went to Ballston, NY in 1783, to Paris [NY] in 1795, to Pompey in 1801, to Volney in 1816, and died in LeRoy, Aug. 26, 1826. His wife was Sarah Ball of Granville, born Nov. 25, 1763.

DANIEL COLE - (See Lafayette) Applied 1831 age 76 yrs. He served in the Rhode Island Continentals.

JOHN COLE - (See Manlius) Applied 1831, age 72 yrs. [In] New York Continentals.

JONATHAN CONKLIN - (See Onondaga) Applied 1831, age 73 yrs. (In] New York Continentals.

SAMUEL CONKLIN - (See Marcellus) Applied 1831 age 66 yrs. of age. New York Militia.

DANIEL CONNER - (See Fabius) Died May 28, 1831.

LEMUEL COOK - Applied 1818, age 58 yrs. [In] Conn. Line from Watertown, 1781-1783 in Sheldon's Dragoons, a farmer, 5 ft. 5 inches high and dark [complexion].

LEMUEL COOK - Served in Canada expedition under Capt. Isaac Cook of Wallingford, CT, being discharged Nov. 20, 1775. Both pensioners were here at the same time. The former applied for a pension a week before the latter and was five years younger.

SELAH COOK - Pompey pioneer and probable veteran, but with no date of death. Possible service in Capt. Smith's company, enlisting April 15, 1775, and going to German Flats, NY. Then he was in Col. Sheldon' Conn. Dragoons, March 22, 1782, enlisting for 3 years. He was from Watertown, CT, a farmer, 5 feet, 7 1/2 inches high, with dark eyes and brown hair. In 1790 he was in Whitesboro, NY which embraced a vast territory. He may have been Serad Cook, pensioner in Madison Co. close by [Cazenovia], who applied in 1831, age 71 yrs. and who served in Connecticut.

TRUEWORTHY COOK - Pompey pioneer and brother of the last. In Whitestown in 1790. They were among the founders of the Congregational Church in Pompey in 1796 and Lucy and Freelove Cook were their wives. Both men were overseers of highways, but Selah owned no land there and Trueworthy sold his in 1817. The former is not mentioned there after 1802. The latter went to Oswego County where he died

July 29, 1822. He applied for a pension in 1818, age 63 yrs., having served in Capt. Smith's company, Conn. Line for three years from March 31, 1777.

WILLIAM COOK - See Pompey. Applied in 1819. Served in the Conn. Continentals.

AARON COOLEY - Pompey. Sarah Cooley, admns. Feb. 3, 1808. Served in various ways from Petersham. Mass., 17777-1780. In Hampshire Co. [MA] in 1790

DAVID CORNELL - See Van Buren, where by error it [the name] is Daniel. Applied 1818, age 66 yrs., having served in the New York Line.

THOMAS CORY - Camillus. Hannah Cory and Jacob Bacon, admns., Nov. 6, 1804. Served from Weston, Middlesex county, Mass., where he still lived in 1790.

EBENEZER COSTON - born Francestown, 1765, enlisted there May 1782 in Capt. Isaac Frye's company. Transferred to Washington's Life Guard, June 16, 1783. This was made up of tall men. He was discharged Dec. 20, 1783, and died in Lysander, NY, Feb. 17, 1814. His wife, Sarah J. Hale, was born in Beverly, NH, June 1, 1763, and died in Sherburne, NY, March 26, 1857.

EBENEZER COLVILLE - See Onondaga. Served in Conn. Continentals.

AMOS C. COWLES - (See Otisco). Younger than the veteran, whose age is unknown, but he presided at the organization of the Washington Religious Society, Otisco, Oct. 1, 1804, and was one of the original trustees.

BENJAMIN COWLES - (See Otisco) The wife's epitaph follows: "In memory of Luvina, wife of Benjamin Cowles who died Jan. 27, 1834, aged 68 yrs."
"So Jesus slept, God's dying son
Passed thro' the grave and bless'd the bed.
Rest here blest soul till from his throne
The morning breaks and frees the dead."

VINE COY - (See Salina) Applied 1831, age 67 yrs. In Capt. Durkee's Co., CT, Aug. 1782-1783. Pensioner in Madison county in 1835.

JOHN CROSS - (See Fabius) Applied 1831 - age 6a9 yrs. In Mass. Militia.

PETER CUDDEBACK - Skaneateles. Jacobus DePuy and Moses Cuddeback, admns, April 5, 1803. In Mamakating, [Sullivan Co.] NY in 1790. Enrolled in Pawling's Levies and the the 2nd Ulster regiment.

PHILLIP CUMMINGS - An old cemetery south of Tully village has this: In Memory of Phillip Cummings who died March 26, 1826, aged 80 yrs." The name is in the 4th

Albany regiment, and another enlisted from Hollis, Mass., May 1, 1775, under Capt. Reuben Dow. This veteran was born in Groton, Mass., Nov. 26, 1745, and served in Hollis where he married Mary Carter, born Nov. 15, 1751, died Oct. 2, 1815.

JOHN CUNNINGHAM - Manlius. Will, May 16, 1814 - July, 1815. He had several grandchildren, and the name is frequent in New England and New York rolls.

ELLIS CURTIS - Onondaga. Alanson Parsons, admns., June 11, 1806. Stratford, CT, Col. Canfield's regiment, 1781 with service at West Point.

ZACHARIA CURTIS - Camillus. Will, July 25, 1822 - Oct. 28, 1823. Wife, Zuba. Many children and grandchildren. The name is in several Mass. regiments, 1779-1783. Probable.

PERES CUSHMAN - Applied 1831, age 74 yrs. Various services in the Mass. Militia, Middleborough, 1777-1779.

JEREMIAH DALY - Fabius. Sarah Daly and James Pettit, admns., Aug. 29, 1815. Name in Col. John Glover's regiment, Mass., 1775-1776. Probable.

MARKS (MARX) DAMUTH - Manlius. Alvin Marsh, admns., March 11, 1813. Tryon county, 4th regiment, and still in Montgomery [Co.] in 1790.

SAMUEL DAVENPORT - Marcellus. Will, Oct. 18, 1809 - Sept. 24, 1811. Three sons and three married daughters. Name in Col. Lemuel Robinson's regiment, Lexington alarm and various services till 1779. Probable.

NATHAN DAVIS - A Revolutionary pensioner of 1792. Several in Mass. rolls.

ELISHA DEAN - Tully. Anson Dean, Cazenovia, admns. Sept. 14, 1816. Col. Daggett's regiment, Easton, Mass 1776 and 1778.

WILLIAM DEAN - Pompey. Will, July 29, 1835 - April 7, 1836. Died Feb. 1, 1836, "an old man." Wife, Anna. Children, Sally, wife of David Husted of Onondaga, Rial and others. Name in Conn. rolls and Dutchess Co., NY. Probable.

JOHN DE GRAFT - Applied 1831, age 72 yrs. First Albany Regiment.

REUBEN DELANO - Skaneateles. Will, Jan. 25, 1830 - June 19 [1830?]. His wife, Joanna, and several children survived him. She died there Oct. 3, 1843, age 86 years, 7 months. All the heirs lived in New York and he seems [to be] thr one enrolled in the 4th Albany L. B. R. regiment. A Minute man born in Duxbury, Mass., June 6, 1761, seems younger. Indications are that our subject was born in Sharon, CT, in 1755, but lived and served in New York.

DAVIS DEMMING - Applied 1831, age 71 years. Served in Conn. Line. He was inspector of elections in Marcellus, 1801-1806.

ABSALOM DENNY - (See Manlius) Applied 1831, age 70 yrs. In Conn. Continentals.

BENJAMIN DE PUY - See Lysander and Van Buren. Applied 1831, age 68 yrs., differing widely from the stone. Service in NY State troops.

JOHN DE PUY - Applied 1831, age 70 yrs. NY Militia.

THOMAS DODGE - Fifer in New Hampshire Line. Applied 1818 age 57 yrs.

ELIJAH DRAKE - (See Skaneateles) Ensign in New York Militia.

SAMUEL DRAPER - Applied 1831, age 72 yrs. Mass. Militia.

JAMES DUNHAM - (See Van Buren) New Jersey Line. Applied 1818, age 62 yrs.

JEREMIAH DUNHAM - (See Camillus) Mass. Line. Applied 1831, age 61 yrs.

CYRIL EATON - Applied 1831, age 66 yrs. Conn. Militia. No record found.

ELEAZER EATON - Applied 1831, age 68 yrs. Willett's New York Levies.

STEPHEN EATON - (See Pompey) Applied 1831, age 68 yrs.

SAMUEL EDWARDS - See Manlius, but may not be the same. Conn. Continentals. Applied 1833 age 76 yrs..

ROBERT ELLIOTT - Onondaga. Will, Nov. 7, 1811 - July 23, 1817. Wife, Prudence and two adult children. Name in 2nd and 3rd Westchester regiment. Also in Mass. Continentals, 1780. In 1790 in Bedford, Westchester county. Probable.

ALEXANDER ENOS - Applied 1831, age 79 yrs. Mass. Militia. No record.

WILLIAM ETZ - Applied 1831, age 69 yrs. First Tryon county L. B. R. regiment. This inscription appears in Preble village cemetery: "Mrs. Elizabeth, wife of Capt. William Etz, died Jan. 31, 1836, age 62 y."

ISAAC FARNAM - Onondaga Hill. Died Oct. 3, 1813, age 49 yrs. His wife, Mehitabel, died Pine Ridge, near Navarino, April 22, 1854, aged 89 yrs."

REUBEN FARNHAM - (See Skaneateles) This pensioner died Aug. 25, 1826.

PAUL FAY - Postoffice tablet. No record found.

WILLIAM FAY - (See Onondaga) Applied 1818, age 67 yrs. In Conn. Line.

CAPT. JOHN FITCH - (See Syracuse) Great grandfather of Hon. Charles E. Fitch, who says; " Capt. John Fitch, the 5th in descent from Rev. James Fitch of Norwich, Conn., was born in Lisbon CT, July 2, 1749, married March 5, 1772, Irene, daughter of Timothy Warner of Windham. He was a farmer, removing to the town of Kirkland, Oneida county, early in the 19th century. He died there Aug. 8, 1840. His wife died Nov. 1, 1817. He was Deputy Commissary General in the Revolutionary war. vide, pages 143 and 430 in Connecticut in the Revolutionary War. Many years ago my father, Thomas B. Fitch, had the remains of Capt. Fitch and wife brought to his lot in Oakwood [cemetery in Syracuse] where they remain." Pensioner in Kirkland, NY, 1840, aged 90 yrs.

JAMES FLETCHER - Applied 1818, no age given. Service in 1st and 3rd NY Line.

GEORGE FOLTS - Applied in 1833, age 80 yrs. In 3rd Regiment of Tryon county. In 1790 in Herkimer.

ELKANAH FULLER - Applied 1818, age 69 yrs. In Col. Ashley's regiment, Mass., from Marlborough in 1780, for 3 yrs, and then aged 18, dark, and 5 feet 1 inch high, not agreeing with pension age.

JOSEPH GANNETT - On Post Office tablet and said to be of Syracuse.. Applied 1831, age 73 yrs. In Capt. David Kingman's company, Mass. Militia for 11 days in 1780. In 1790 in Bridgewater, Mass.

SAMUEL GILBERT - (See Camillus) Applied 1831, age 73 yrs. He served in Conn. Continentals.

WILLIAM GILLCHRISS - Onondaga. Timothy Gillchriss and Chauncey Rust, admns. Oct. 27, 1803. Fourth NY Line. He came to Salina in 1793 and kept a tavern there, a favorite life for old soldiers.

NATHAN GOODALL - (See Fabius) Applied 1818, age 70 yrs. Died 29, 1831.

JOSEPH GOODELL - (See Tully) In the same ruined cemetery is his wife's name: "Elizabeth Goodell, died May 22, 1856, in the 85th year of her age." Probable.

JACOB GOODRICH - (See Fabius) He applied for a pension from Fabius, Sept. 11, 1832 and was then 78 [years of age]. The claim was allowed. April 1775, he enlisted for nine months in Capt. Dibble's company, Col. Patterson's regiment, Mass. for one month, 1777 in Capt. Oliver Belden's company being called out on several alarms. He then lived in Lenox, Mass.

WINTHROP GRAHAM - Will made in Marcellus, March 2, 1803. Wife, Rebekah, and his mother, Elizabeth Child, survived him with ten children. Three of his daughters were married. Winthrop Graham served in Capt. Parmelee Allen's company, VT, for three weeks in 1781, and afterward in the same year, for two weeks in Capt. Asaph Cook's company. In 1790 he was in Washington Co., NY.

DAVID GREEN - "Died July 22, 1848 in the 87th year of his age. I have fought the good fight, I have finished my course. I have kept the faith henceforth there is laid up for me a crown of righteousness."
Hannah, wife of David Green, "Died Apr. 22, 1838 in the 82 yr. of her age. Blessed are the dead which die in the Lord."
Pompey Center. A family record said he was born in Connecticut in 1769. He married Hannah Pease in 1796 and came to Green's Corners [now Pompey Center] from New Milford the same year. The name is in many rolls. In some ways the best identification is in Falmouth, Mass, under Capt. Palmer, 1778 and Capt. Clark, 1780. Age then 19, height 5 feet 6 inches, complexion light. The place is an objection. One was a lieutenant in Capt. Averill's company, New Milford, 1782. Probably the last if a veteran.

ENOS GREENFIELD - (See Pompey) Pensioner died Nov. 23, 1824.

DAVID GROOM - Marcellus. Hannah Groom and others admns. Feb. 4, 1801. The name is in the 12th Albany regiment and in Halfmoon in 1790. Probable.

EZEKIEL GOVES - Applied 1831, age 85 yrs. In Conn. Militia, but lacking record.

STEPHEN HAGER - (See Marcellus) Applied 1818, age 62 yrs. In Mass. Line. Died Nov. 22, 1822.

EPHRAIM HALL - See Onondaga. This pensioner served in the Mass. Militia.

JABESH HALL - Marcellus. Delila Hall, admns. Feb. 22, 1813. Name in Mass. Continentals., 1782, for 9 months. Probable.

GEORGE HANSEL - In Klock's New York regiment. Pensioned Sept. 22, 1786 and probably served at Oriskany.

GAIUS M. HARMON - (See Elbridge) Mary, his wife, was appointed administrator, June 27, 1807.

SOLOMON HATCH - Manlius. Lois Hatch and Samuel Messenger, Jr. admns., July 17, 1804. Four of the name served in Mass., but none were there in 1790. In Weissenfels' NY Levies, and in 1790 in Albany Co. Probable.

ROBERT HEBBARD - Pompey. Will, Sept. 27, 1817 - Nov. 12 [1817]. Wife, Leah, with three sons and three married daughters. Name in Dutchess county 6th L. B. R regiment. in 1790 Amenia, NY. Probable.

EPHRAIM HEWITT - Applied 1831, age 71 yrs. In Berkshire Militia, Mass., 1777 and 1780.

LEONARD HOAR - Aaron C. Hoar, admns., May 12, 1814. Two of this name served in the Mass. troops and were still there in 1790. Probable.

JOHN HOLLISTER - Salina. Phebe Hollister, admns. Dec. 11, 1813. In Conn. troops in 1776, under Capt. Hale and Capt. Mills.

HENDRICK HOOS - Applied 1818. From Addison, VT. In Mass. Line, 1777-1783. In Sheffield, described as aged 38 in 1783, and 5 feet 8 inches high.

ELI HOPKINS - Fabius. Abner Hopkins, admns. Feb. 28, 1805. Fourth NY Line. In 1790, Washington county, NY.

DAVID HORTON - Fabius. Will, April 6, 1807 - Aug. 7, 1813. Wife, Willibee. Also children and grandchildren. Frequent in NY troops and in 1790. Probable. Deacon in First Congregational Society at organization in 1808.

PHINEAS HOWELL - "To the memory of Phineas Howell, who died June 15th, 1809 in the 67th year of his age after eight days severe illness in Tully, NY." "Phebe, widow of Phineas Howell died Sept 2, 1836 in the 93 year of her age." Tully village cemetery. Will June 7, 1809-July 6 [1809]. Beside wife, 5 sons and 3 daughters survived him. His son, Floyd was born in 1777. He served in the 4th Orange Co. regiment, and was still there in 1790. Prominent citizen.

EZEKIEL HOYT - Applied 1831, age 73 yrs. Died Aug. 19, 1832. Served in Conn. Militia, but no record appears.
The simple epitaph in the LaFayette cemetery reads: "Ezekiel Hoyt, 1753-1834." "Mary, his wife, 1764-1834."

DAVID HUNTER - Applied 1818, age 71 yrs. Served in Mass Line. Several of the name.

SOLOMON HUNTLEY - See Camillus. His first wife, Rebecca, left children.

COL. JEREMIAH JACKSON - (See Pompey) He died on lot 61, near Onativa [east of village of Lafayette - just off Rt. 20].

JACOB T. JOHNSON - Tully. Will Feb. 17, 1817 - May 3 [1817]. His wife, Esther and eight children survived him. A frequent name in NY and New England rolls. Probable.

SAMUEL JONES - (See Pompey) Applied in 1831. Served in Conn. Militia.

JONATHAN P. JUDD - Onondaga. Dorcas Judd, admns., Jan. 29, 1813. Jonathan Judd served from Guilford, CT in the Lexington alarm and was still there in 1790. Probable.

BENAJAMIN JUNE - (See LaFayette) This pensioner served in the Mass. Militia.

DAVID KEELER - Applied 1818, age 60 yrs. Served in Conn. Line and died March 11, 1822.

ELIJAH KEELER - Onondaga. Isaac Keeler and Nathan Brown, admns. March 16, 1802. With Capt. Asa Barns, June 30, 1775, and sergeant under Capt. David Wheeler, Mass. Oct. 1780.

THOMAS KEENEY - Fabius, and in previous list. He applied in 1831, age 81 yrs. and served in Conn. Militia. The First Baptist Society of Fabius was organized in his house, Nov. 21, 1806.

BARAK KEITH - "In memory of Barak Kieth, who died March 26, 1833, aged 70 years & 7 months."
"Beneath this stone till Christ shall bid him rise
A much loved Husband, Father, Brother lies.
In vain were tears, death came at heaven's command
Cease then each murmur at the sovereign hand."

"In memory of Matilda, wife of B. Kieth, who died Jan. 31, 1836, aged 64 yrs."
Applied 1831, aged 71, not as on stone. Served in Conn. Militia, but not found on rolls. In 1790 in Thompson, CT. Interred in Oran [town of Pompey] cemetery.

PAUL KING - Pompey. Will, Dec. 31, 1807 - Jan. 29, 1809. Wife, Mary. Of his three sons, Apollos and Orange were soldiers, and Paul, the eldest, was probably one. The name is in Col. Dickerson's Mass. regiment, 1777, and as First Lieutenant under Col. Chapin, 1779. Both father and son were in Chesterfield, MA in 1790. No tombstones have been found, but they did not live in Pompey. Paul King, Jr., died in Pompey, Feb. 1810, leaving a wife, Hannah and six children.

MOSES KNAPP - applied 1831, age 68 yrs. Served in NY Militia.

JOHN LADLOW - See Otisco. This pensioner died Dec. 25, 1822.

BENJAMIN LAMPSON - (See Onondaga) Applied 1831. Service in Conn. Line

ARIEL LAWRENCE - (See Marcellus) The one who died in 1807 was Ariel, Jr., his will being witnessed by Ariel, Sen. In 1824 the latter was still a member of Morning Star Lodge, Marcellus, F. & A. M., but no record of his death is available.

ELIJAH LAWRENCE - Onondaga. Roxe Lawrence and Medad Curtis, admns., Oct. 16, 1800. Enlisted from Canaan, CT, March 1, 1780, and also in Capt. Chapman's Company, Jan. 1, 1781 - Dec. 31, 1781.

HENRY LANSING - Applied 1831, age 70 yrs. and died Jan. 28, 1833. Served in NY Continentals.

CHRISTOPHER LEACH - Lysander. Sheldon Logan of Onondaga, admns., May 20, 1801. Served in Lt. Col. Stevens' NY Artillery, from Lyme, CT, and also in 1775 in Connecticut. He drew lot 51 in Lysander.

JOSEPH LEAVITT - (See DeWitt) This pensioner applied in 1831 and was sergeant and ensign in Conn. Militia.

JOHN LEFEVER - Skaneateles. Will June 21, 1814 - Feb. 20, 1815. He left a wife, not named, three sons and four daughters. The youngest son was born in 1787. The father lived on lot 85. His name is in the 4th regiment of Orange county, and in one of Ulster [Co.] where he still lived in 1790.

JAMES LEONARD - Pompey. Will, Oct. 2, 1815 - Oct. 10 [1815]. His wife, Eunice survived him, with 3 sons, 4 married daughters and many grandchildren. Many of the name in NY and N.E. [New England] rolls. In 1790 in Thompson, CT. Interred in Oran cemetery [town of Pompey]. Probable.

EZRA LOOMIS - In Camillus in 1807. Applied in 1831, age 80 yrs.

ENOS LUDDEN - Applied 1831, age 73 yrs. Various services in Mass. Militia, 1779-1783.

LUTHER MANLEY - "Hannah, wife of Luther Manley, died Oct. 7, 1835, aged 78 years. Thorn Hill cemetery. See Marcellus.

ELIJAH MANN - "Died Mar. 15, 1836, aged 85 yrs." "Ruby, his wife, Oct. 15, 1828, aged 75 years." Onondaga Hill. The name is in Capt. Amidon's company, Col. Dean's Mass. Regiment, March 4, 1781, for 14 days. Also in Champion, CT, Nov. 24, 1776, for the war, and as a corporal in Capt. John H. Buell's company, 1781. In 1790 only in Barre, Mass. Probable.

WILLIAM MAPES - Applied 1831, age 78 yrs. Sergeant in Orange and Ulster Militia, NY.

GURDON MARCHANT - Cayuga Co. pensioner in 1835, and may not have lived here, but his wife's stone in Chase's Cemetery in Lysander, reads: "Hannah, wife of Gordon Merchant, died Aug. 28, 1847, aged 85 years, 3 mos. and 8 days. " (Verse) Applied 1831, age 74 yrs. He served in the Conn. Continentals.

PATRICK MC GEE - (See Clay) He is in the list of 1835, applying in 1818, age 57. Service in the Penn. Line. This adds much to our knowledge of this early pioneer. Town meeting was held at his tavern in 1805.

JOSEPH MC MILLAN - See Pompey. He died May 15, 1826.

JOHN MEEKER - "Died July 3rd, 1840, in his 73 year. This Monument erected by his Widow & Children." "Theodocia, Wife of John Meeker, Died April 23d, 1834, in her 67 year. This Monument is Erected by Her Children.
Family lot on Meeker Hill, Tully. See Tully, but his age makes service doubtful. Newspaper accounts made him older. His widow, Eliza, whom he married soon after his [1st] wife's death, had children buried there, but little could be gained form the broken stones, and less from the field stones marking other graves.

CHARLES MERRIMAN - See Otisco. His wife's stone reads: "In memory of Rachel, wife of Charles Merriman, who died Sept. 10, 1826, aged 69 years."

JOHN MIDDLEBROOK - Died Aug. 25, 1836, age 71 yrs." "Our Mother, Abigail Middlebrook, died Aug. 30, 1852, ae 84 yrs."
"Farewell, Mother, here rests thy head
Beneath kind natures's lowly bed;
Sweetly sings thy spirit blest
Crowned in Heaven thy long sought rest."

With his wife, this pensioner rests in the old cemetery [in] Fabius village. He applied in 1831, age 68 yrs, differing from stone. Conn. Militia, but not in rolls.

PETER MILLER - (See Salina) Applied 1831, age 76 yrs.. In NY Militia, but if the dates supplied are correct this would require two of the same name, as seems unlikely.

SOLOMON MOREY - "In Memory of Solomon Morey, who died Nov. 20th, 1815, aged 53 years, & 8 months, 28 days.
"Adieu my friends, dry up your tears
I must lie here till Christ Appears"

Prostrate and broken stone, the only engraved one in the small burial lot on the farm once owned by him, on lot 38, Pompey, between Jamesville and Pompey Hill. Part of the name is gone, but his will is in the Surrogate's office as was proved April 29, 1816. Israel Sloan had been named as executor, but Morey's wife, Jerusha, took his place. He then had married children. The name is in Vermont rolls of 1781 in Capt. Smith's company of Fairlee, for short service, and he was still there in 1790.

CHARLES MORGAN - [On] Post Office tablet. Some promised notes did not come. Early engaged in making salt, he is said to have been buried on his farm near the Morgan church in Clay. The name is in Conn. rolls from Hartford.

EBENEZER MORELY - See Van Buren. The 1835 list gives the name of Maley, application 1818 age 76 yrs. while his application in 1820 made him but 64 yrs. His wife's stone in Warner cemetery reads: "In Memory of Prudence, Wife of Ebenezer Morely, who died June 26, 1838. Ae. 77 yr's."

ASA MORRILL - Applied 1818, age 72 yrs. Col. John Ashley, Mass. Line, July 22 - Aug. 13, 1777.

JOHN MOSS - Onondaga. Mary Clarina Moss, admns., Nov. 13, 1816. A frequent name in NY and New England rolls. Apparently the one who was elected warden of St. John's Church, 1803, and of Zion Church, 1816, Onondaga Hill. Probable.

MOSES MOULTROUP - "Died Mar. __, 1848, aged 84 years." "Ann, Wife of Moses Moultroup, Died June 24, 1831, aged 63 years." See Pompey. A pensioner. These stones were overlooked in a former hasty visit to the Pompey Center cemetery.

JESSE NEWELL - Camillus. Levi Clark, admns., Aug. 28, 1819. Private in Col. Brooks regiment, Mass., Nov. 5, 1777-Apr. 3, 1778.

JOHN NEWELL - Applied 1831, age 88 yrs. Mass. Continentals.

CHRISTOPHER NORTON - Same year [1831], age 72 yrs. Albany county, 6th regiment.

JAMES OLCOTT - Pompey. Hoahdiah and Lebbus Olcott, admns., March 21, 1815. In Lieut. Bidwell's company, CT, in 1776, in NY campaign.

TIMOTHY OLCOTT - Pompey. Hezekiah Olcott, admns. Sept. 23, 1797. In Capt. David Smith's company, Waterbury, CT. in 1776, and went to German Flats, NY with his company.

JAMES OLMSTEAD - Applied 1831, age 78 yrs. Died Feb. 16, 1834. Lieutenant in Conn. Continentals, Capt. Dorrance, from East Hartford, Dec. 24, 1778 - Nov 20, 1882.

COL. DAVID OLMSTED - See DeWitt. The inference from the tombstone that he had a second wife is erroneous. In his will he gives to his daughter, Abigail certain bedding "after her mamma has made her selection." His wife, Abigail, four sons and three daughters survived him.

PETER OLNEY - He enlisted in Sept. 1775 and Aug. 1777 being at first under Col. Samuel Stafford, in 1777 he enlisted at Killingly, CT and 1781 in Adams, Mass. In LaFayette, NY Sept. 8, 1832, he applied for a pension, the claim being allowed. He was born in Smithfield, RI Nov. 21, 1750 and lived in Providence till 1760, marrying Tabitha Clark in Killingly, CT Dec. 23, 1773 and died Feb. 16, 1834. His widow secured a pension March 7, 1837, being then 8r years old and living in LaFayette. He was in the battle of Bennington. No stones observed.

DANIEL OWEN - See Spafford. This pensioner died May 22, 1826.

JOHN PADDOCK - Applied 1831, age 6a8 yrs. Willett's Levies and 1st NY Line. Probably of Camillus.

DAVID PALMER - Camillus. Dameras Palmer, admns. Mar. 27, 1817. In NY and New England rolls. Probable.

CHARLES PARDEE - See Skaneateles. Applied 1831, age 72 yrs. Served in Conn. Militia.

JOHN PARKE - See Manlius. Applied 1818 and died the following year. Sergeant in the Conn. Line.

ELIAS PARKER - Pompey, July 25, 1815. Elidiey (Lydia) Parker became admns. He was a Lieutenant in Col. Crane's Artillery, etc. 1777-1780, in Massachusetts.

LIEUT. ELI PARSONS - This veteran was born near Springfield, Mass, Jan. 29, 1748, and married Persis Graves, June 5, 1777, who was born in 1755. He was in Col. Lieutenant John Crane's Artillery, through most of the war. He shared in Shay's rebellion, afterward living in Cherry Valley and Canajoharie where he was in 1790. He then went to Manlius and thence to Oswego, before 1812, where he died Sept. 25, 1830. Pensioner.

SILAS PEASE - "In Memory of Silas Pease, a Revolutionary Soldier, who departed this life on the 21st of March 1836, in the 77th year of his age.
    "Here rests the man who dared be free;
    He periled his life for liberty;
    At Bunker Hill he took the field,
    And at Yorktown, saw the Britan yield."

"Dorcas Curtis, wife of Silas Pease, Born June 2, 1776, Died April 28, 1854." Fleming Cemetery, Cayuga County. See Skaneateles. The stone makes him older than the obscure family history.

EBENEZER PEARCE - See Fabius. He was born in Rhode Island, Feb. 17, 1731 and in 1790 was in Hancock, Mass. Wife, Elizabeth.

JOSEPH PECK -(See Onondaga) His wife's epitaph is here added from the Valley cemetery:
"In Memory of Mrs. Hannah, wife of Capt. Joseph Peck who died Sept. 5th, 1839, Aged 83 yrs. The Lord my Righteousness"

SIMON PHARIS - (See Onondaga) Andrew [Pharis?] became his admns. May 4, 1817, antedating common records nearly three years. Accurate dates are thus slowly evolved.

JOHN PHELPS - Applied 1819, age 61 yrs. Mass. Line

NOAH PHELPS - Fabius. Oliver Phelps, admns., June 27, 1804. Several of this name served in Conn. troops. Probable.

PETER PINNEY - Onondaga. Will, April 8, 1813 - April 16 [1813]. Wife, Olive but no children. Name in Capt. Willes' company, Tolland, CT, May 7 - Dec. 17, 1777. No record as head of family in 1790.

CHARLES PITTS - Postoffice tablet. No record in accessible rolls.

IRA POMEROY - (See Otisco) Applied 1831, age 74 yrs. In Conn. Militia.

CALEB POTTER - (See Onondaga) This pensioner first applied in 1831, age 69 yrs. Served in the R. I. Militia.

NATHANIEL POTTER - Fabius. Allen Potter of Argyle, NY, admns. Sept 11, 1801. Albany county, 13th regiment.This seems a good identification, but the name was frequent, with and without service.

CALEB PRATT - Applied in 1831, age 72 yrs, and served in Vermont Militia. He came to Manlius in 1793.

NOAH PRATT - This Onondaga Co. veteran was in Col. Sprout's regiment for four years, and well remembered Joy Babbitt there till his own discharge in June 1783.

SAMUEL PRICE - Pompey. Darkes (Dorcas) Price, admns., Sept. 29, 1800. Several in CT and NY. Probable.

DAVID QUACKENBUSH - Applied in 1831, age 73 yrs., Corporal in N. Y. Continentals, Tryon Co.

JAMES QUIGLEY - Applied 1828, age 75 yrs. Served under Col. Groton, Mass. Line, 1777-1780.

ABRAHAM RAYMOND - Pompey. Will, Jan. 14, 1813 - April 9 [1813]. Wife, Isabella, with 3 sons and 3 minor grandchildren. Name in Capt. Eli Reed's company, Conn. Line, from Norwalk. There and Kinderhook, NY in 1790. Probable.

EBENEZER REDFIELD - Camillus. Tamer Redfield, admns., March 25, 1819. Deerfield, Mass., Col. John Moseley. Probable.

HENRY REES - Manlius. Jacob Rees, admns., Aug. 8, 1820. Albany Co., 8th regiment. Probable.

DANIEL REED - Camillus. Mary and William Reed, admns., Dec. 6, 1802. A frequent name in rolls, and thus possible.

THOMAS REWEY - See Van Buren. Applied in 1831, age 81 yrs. and reported service in New York Militia.

CHARLES RICHARDS - Marcellus. Will, Feb. 12k 1817 - June 23, 1820. Eight children and some grandchildren. Name in Vermont rolls, in Col. Williams' regiment, 1777 and Capt Jonathan Hatton's company, 1780. Only in Conn. in 1790. Probable.

DANIEL RICHARDSON - [On] P. O. tablet. The name occurs in Lexington alarm, Attleborough, Mass, and in Col. Dagget's regiment, 1776. One also served from Woburn in the Lexington alarm in Capt. Jonathan Fox's company. In 1790 in Attleborough and elswhere.

JOSIAH RICHMOND - See Salina. He was born in Dighton, Mass., May 1747 and died in Salina May 28, 1821. As a prisoner in the Revolution, he was taken to Bermuda. He married Betsey Hathaway, born 1750, died 1835.

HENRY RICHTMEYER - Applied 1831, age 70 yrs, and was then in Madison county. In rolls it is Rightmire. He also had a pension in 1815. Mr. Van Antwerp, a descendant sends notes, saying he was on the staff of W. G. Fuller as aide-de-camp, settled in Kirkville or Mycenae, married __ Shaver, and was buried on his farm. She thinks there is a stone. His name appears as a private in Col. Willett's Levies. The only W. Fuller reported in NY troops was also a private.

BENJAMIN RIDER - Manlius. Asahel Hawley, admns., Aug. 26, 1811. In NY and Mass. rolls. Possible, which might be said of many others, the appointment of administrators having by slight indications of age.

PELHAM RIPLEY - See DeWitt. Applied in 1831 and served in Mass. Militia.

ISSACHAR ROBINSON - Applied same year [as above] and served in NY Continentals.

NATHAN ROBINSON - Applied 1831, age 74 yrs. Served in Mass. Militia.

THOMAS ROBINSON - [On] P. O. tablet. Many in rolls. Administrators for two here in 1816 and 1817.

MOSES ROGERS - Applied 1831, age 71 yrs. Dubois' NY Levies and 2nd Ulster Regiment, Inspector of elections in Camillus, 1804-05.

EDWARD ROSS - (See Otisco) Applied 1831, age 76 yrs. Musician in Rhode Island Militia.

THOMAS ROUSE - [Applied] same year [as above] age 91 yrs. Died Nov. 25, 1832. In Col. Simmonds' Berkshire Militia, Mass., 27 days in 1777.

DAVID ROWLAND - (See Fabius) [Applied] same year, age 70 yrs. but assigned to Conn Militia.

JAMES SACKETT - [Applied] same year, age 72 yrs.; died Sept. 1, 1833. Westchester and Dutchess Co. regiments.

SILAS SCOFIELD - (See Lysander) Applied 1831, age 74 yrs.

SELAH SCOFIELD - Pensioner, Dec. 8, 1788. Webb's Conn. Continentals.

JOHN SCOTT 3rd - (See Camillus) Applied 1818, age 71 yrs. Died Sept. 1, 1831. Served in the Conn. Line.

DAVID SCOVILLE - (See Pompey) His second wife, Esther, survived him, and he left many married children.

DANIEL SCOVILLE - He was accidentally given as a pensioner of 1840, which is an error.

JAMES SECOR - Applied 1831, age 88 yrs. Died Feb. 14, 1834. In the 3rd Orange Regiment.

EBENEZER SEELEY - Marcellus. Winston Day, admns., May 9, 1798. Several in New York and Conn. rolls. In 1790 [in] Norwalk, CT. In Skaneateles paper is a notice of the death of Mrs. Seeley, mother of Anson S., who died March 14, 1846, age 85 yrs, and who seems to be the widow.

SAMUEL SHERMAN - See Manlius. Applied in 1831, age 76 yrs.

JOHN SHIELDS - See Pompey. Error. According to family history he came from Ireland after the war.

GEORGE SHULTS - "Died Sept. 7, 1840, Ae 83 yrs & 3 mo."
" The Lord is good, a strong hold in the day of trouble and he knoweth them that trust him."

"In Memory of Catharine, wife of George Shuts [sic] who died Sept. 12th, 1830 aged 70 years."

Manlius Center. Applied 1831, age 74 yrs. NY Militia, but no record appears. Received pension in 1833.

SAMUEL SIMPSON - Camillus. Benjamin Simpson, admns. Sept. 24, 1806. Name in Newcastle, Mass., 1776-1777; various services. Probable.

JOSEPH SIVER - [On] P. O. tablet. Not found in rolls but a Joseph Sevey in NH rolls and census of 1790 may be this veteran. In one of the Cicero cemeteries is a Joseph Siver.

AMOS SKEEL - This pensioner is in the Cortland list of 1835, having applied in 1831, age 67 yrs. He served in the Mass. Militia, and was inspector of elections in Fabius in 1804-05 and in Tully in 1806. He died Oct. 4, 1841, age 75 yrs. and his wife, Bethiah [died] Oct. 2, 1853, age 88 yrs. Both rest in Preble Village cemetery.

SIMEON SKEELS - (See Skaneateles) Applied 1819, age 64 yrs. Died Jan 14, 1823.

BERIAH SKINNER - Applied 1818, age 58 yrs.. Capt. in Conn. Line, April 7 1777 - April 1780 and July - DEc. 1780.

JONATHAN SKINNER - Pompey. Jerusha and Jonathan Skinner, admns. Dec. 27, 1808. Willett's NY Levies, and in Connecticut.

ITHMAR SMITH - Applied 1831, age 77. Mass. Militia.

REUBEN SNIFFEN - See LaFayette. Applied in 1831, age 85 yrs.

DAVID SOWL - [Applied] same year [as above], age 75 yrs. In Conn. Militia but records not found. Pensioner.

JOHN SPARLING - See Manlius. Died July 14, 1827. Pensioner.

JEREMIAH SPENCER - Marcellus. Son, Ebenezer, admns. Sept. 29, 1796. Two records in Mass. 1777 and 1780 may mean one man.

ANDREW SNRAGUE -[sic] [May be Sprague] Applied in 1831, age 80 yrs. Sergeant in 2nd Ulster regiment.

ANDREW SPRAGUE - Applied in 1831, aged 80 yrs. Sergeant Mass. Line.

JONATHAN STANLEY - Fabius. Will, Mar. 19, 1805 - Jan. 1814. Wife, Jerusha. Three sons and three married daughters. He was a member of the Assembly in 1812. One of the name had frequent service in Mass. Probable.

ASA STARKWEATHER - Pompey. Will Dec. 8, 1809 - April 16, 1810. Wife, Adah and four children. He bought 100 acres on lot 12 in 1794. Name under Capt. Morgan in 1776, and Capt. Belcher in Stonington, CT in 1777. Probable.

GEORGE STATENGER - Applied 1818, age 68 yrs. Died May 6, 1819. Stoutenger in NY Line and records of death, Manlius. Mary Elizabeth, his widow survived.

ISRAEL STRONG - [Applied] same year [as above], age 76 yrs. Lieut. in Conn. Line. East Windsor, 1777-1781.

SOLOMON SUTHERLAND - Pompey. Will, Nov. 30, 1807 - Jan. 11, 1808. Wife, Lois and four children. Name in 6th Dutchess regiment. Not head of family in 1790. Probable.

WILLIAM SWAIN - Phylura Swain, admns. Dec. 3, 1812. Name in 13th Albany L. B. R. regiment, and also in Mass. Probable. In Albany Co. in 1790.

LEWIS SWEETING, SR. - The lineage book says he died in Manlius, but family records say his wife was a widow when she came there with her son.

JOHN SWEETING - See Manlius. Family records state that this pensioner came to Manlius with his mother, then a widow in 1793, settling on lot 76. She died before 1809 and he then sold out and went to Westmoreland, being over 50 yrs. old. There is a nice story of his meeting Mary Sessions there, a teacher from Vermont, and of their marriage. He was living in Clinton, NY in 1835 where he died, aged over 90 years.

JOHN SWIFT - (See Fabius) This pensioner applied in 1831, age 81 yrs., having served in Mass. Militia.

ESEK TABER - (See Camillus) This pioneer who died in 1814 left children and grandchildren.

PETER TALLMAN - (See Skaneateles) This pensioner who applied in 1831, age 73 yrs., does not agree in age with either of those recorded, but is the Skaneateles veteran. He application gives service in Conn. Militia.

JOHN D. TAYLOR - [On] P. O. tablet. John Taylor is frequent on the rolls.

RUSSEL TAYLOR - "Died March 17, 1839, aged 79 years 9 Mo. & 3 Ds." "Asenath, wife of Russel Taylor, died April 13, 1843, aged 84 years."
  A Marcellus pioneer and apparently Roswell in the Conn. Militia, in which he served. This appears in Lieut. Seymour's company. His application was in 1831, and age 73 yrs. [Buried?] in Old Cemetery, Marcellus.

STEPHEN THOMPSON - (See Camillus) This pensioner applied in 1818, age 60 yrs., having served in the Conn. Line.

MOSES THORP - Fabius. Will, Dec. 19, 1811 - Dec. 26, 1812. Wife, Sarah. Son, Daniel and three married daughters. Name in Col. Brown's Berkshire Regiment, Mass., serving on the Mohawk. Also in West Springfield and New Marlborough, Mass. in 1790. Probable.

RICHARD TOWNSEND - (See Pompey) Applied 1831, age 74 yrs. in NY Continentals.

ISAAC TROWBRIDGE - (See Skaneateles) Applied 1818, age 80 yrs. Mass. Line. In list of 1835 in Cayuga county.

SAMUEL TULLY - Born in 1750 and died in Tully in 1827. He enlisted in 1777 in NY, and served through the war. His wife was his cousin, Sarah Tully, according to the DAR Lineage Book, and he served in Col. VanSchaick's 1st NY Line.

WOODHULL TURNEUR - Probably Skaneateles. Applied 1831 ae 78 yrs. In NJ Militia, but company not mentioned.

JOHN VAN PATTEN - Tully. Will, Oct. 16, 1824 - Sept. 10, 1825. Wife, Margaret. Four sons and three married daughters. His wife died there Oct. 8, 1851, aged 100 years. The only one in the census of 1790 was in Watervliet, NY, apparently Capt. John V. P., of the 2nd Albany Regiment. It seems a clear identification.

THOMAS VICKERY - Pompey. Abigail Vickery and Ozias Burr, admns. Feb. 28, 1808. Name in 3rd Dutchess Co. regiment, NY and Capt. Ichabod Doolittle's company, [in] 1775, which may be the same. Probable. In 1790 in Montgomery Co., NY.

COLOGUS VINAL - Pompey. Will, Aug. 4, 1823 - Oct 22 [1823]. Wife, Martha with five sons and five daughters. In Lexington Alarm, Scituate, Mass., Capt. Wm. Turner. In 1790 in Chesterfield, Mass. Probable.

THOMAS WAIT - (See Skaneateles) Naomi, his wife, lies beside him in the Mottville cemetery, but the dates are deeply buried.

CORNELIUS WALLACE - Applied 1831, age 68 yrs. In NY Militia, but with no record.

ADAM WALTER - (See Manlius) This pensioner applied in 1831, age 80 yrs, and served in the NY Militia.

EBENEZER WARD - [Applied the] same year [as above]. Served in Conn. Militia. No record.

CHARLES WARNER - [Applied the] same year. See Syracuse.

DAVID WATKINS - Applied 1831, age 65 yrs. (See Pompey) Died July 24, 1827. In Mass Line.

JAMES WATSON - "Died Nov. 27, 1820 in the 67th year of his age." "Mary, Wife of James Watson Died April 21, 1848, aged 87 yrs." [Buried] Mottville cemetery in Skaneateles. 13th Albany regiment and another. In 1790 in Westchester, Co. Probable.

BENJAMIN WEBB - (See LaFayette) Applied 1831, age 75 yrs. Corp. in Conn. Continentals.

SAMUEL WEBSTER - [Applied] the same year [as above], age 75 yrs. (See Fabius). Sergt. in Conn. Continentals.

PETER WELLS - [Applied] same year as above, age 85 yrs., in RI Continentals.

JOHN WEST - (See Skaneateles) [Applied] same year [as above]. Corp. in the NY Militia.

NATHANIEL WESTON - "Died March 11, 1822 in the 85th year of his age." "Mary, wife of Nathaniel Weston, died Jan. 10, 1820 in the 79th year of her age." See Pompey. Two small stones overlooked in the Jamesville cemetery. Name in Mass. rolls. Probable. He was an inspector of elections in Pompey, 1799-1801.

SAMUEL WHEADON - An early settler in Marcellus, was a member of the Presbyterian church there in 1801 but went to Michigan and died there in 1835. The name is in Capt. Douglass's company, Conn., 1775 - 1776, which shared in the Canada campaign. Quite probable.

DAVID WHITE - (See La Fayette) Applied 1831, age 74 yrs. In the Conn. Militia.

JABEZ WHITMORE - "Died Dec. 5, 1843, Ae. 77 Y'rs. 3 Mo. 18 D's."
"He sleeps the sleep that knows no waking,
His last long dreamless sleep,
While hearts in anguish deep are breaking,
And friends in sorrow weep."

"Sally, Wife of Jabez Whitmore, Died Mar. 2, 1862, aged 89 y'rs 2m's & 13 days. Blessed are the pure in heart for they shall see God."

See Pompey for the records, but they are buried in the West Otisco Cemetery.

ISAAC WETHERBEE - See P. O. tablet. In 1780 served in Lunenburgh, Mass. Several of the name later.

DAVID WILLIAMS - (See Manlius) On good authority, I am told he was buried in the tabular tomb in the ruined cemetery, [on] lot 9, Pompey, on or near the David Williams farm.

EBEN WILLIAMS - [On] P. O. tablet. Supplied 1818, age 78 yrs. Lieut. in Mass. Line. In rolls it is always Ebenezer.

JAMES WILLIAMS - Applied 1831, age 77 yrs. in NJ Militia.

GODFREY WILLISTON - (See Pompey) [Applied] same year, age 70 years. Col. Asa Whitcomb's regiment, Mass. Militia in 1776.

SAMUEL WINCHESTER - Marcellus. Will, Jan. 20, 1820 - Feb. 7, 1823. His first wife was Rebeka and there were five sons and two daughters. His second wife, Hannah, also had children. The name appears in the Lexington Alarm from Brookline, Mass. Probable.

REUBEN WOODWARD - Applied 1831, age 68 yrs. In Conn. Continentals, but no record appears.

ENOS WRIGHT - Pompey. Will, Nov. 4, 1805 - Nov. 6, 1806. Wife, Sarah, four sons and two daughters; one of the latter a minor. Son, Ezekiel, born in 1766. Name in Mass. 2nd Line. Two in Connecticut in 1790. Probable.

VETERANS IN MILITARY LODGE, MANLIUS

Those reported by Mr Lakin have already appeared, A few are now added.

EPHRIAM BARRETT - The lodge had "an elegant entertainment" at this brother's house Dec. 17, 1810., but his name is not in Lakin's list of members unless it is Erastus . He served under Capt. Allen in a Conn. company in 1776, and was in Windham, Conn. in 1790.

DANIEL CHASE - This may be one already mentioned in Lysander.

ROBERT CARSKADDEN - He was in the Ulster 4th L.B.R. regiment.

LEMUEL JOHNSON - He served in /capt. Timothy Page's company of Mass., in 1777, and was at Bennington, with later service in 1780. In 1790, he was in Berkshire, Mass.

MOSES LILLEY - In Capt. Pettibone's company, Simsbury, Conn., in 1777 and still there in 1790.

OLIVER W. MILLER - Various services in Berkshire, Mass.

DANIEL OLDS - In Capt. Noble's company, Berkshire, Mass and various to 1780.

CALEB PRATT - Pension, already mentioned.

ANDREW PHARIS - Already recorded and living in salina. Some members were farther away.

JOHN RAPALYEA -In 2nd Dutchess regiment.

TIMOTHY TEALL - Already recorded, but without date of death. June 15, 1820, there was a special lodge meeting to attend his funeral.

SMITH WEED - This early physician was Commissary in Gen. Waterbury's Staff, Conn., in 1781 and in Norwalk in 1790. After some years in Manlius, he went to the northeast part of New York, where he died.

ISAAC WETHERBEE - Already recorded, Mrs. Mary Wetherby, buried at Oran, may have been his wife. She died Oct. 2, 1817, aged 46 years.

POSSIBLE VETERANS IN THIS LODGE WERE:

Thomas Bancroft
John Bowers
Thomas Church
Samuel Foster
        Samuel Woodworth

John Higgins
Benjamin Hutchins
Elijah Kent
Levi Ward

www.ingramcontent.com/pod-product-compliance
Lightning Source LLC
Chambersburg PA
CBHW061315040426
42444CB00010B/2661